A COWBOY'S LIFE

by Joanna Korba
illustrated by Jerry Tiritilli

Scott Foresman
is an imprint of

Glenview, Illinois • Boston, Massachusetts • Chandler, Arizona
Upper Saddle River, New Jersey

Every effort has been made to secure permission and provide appropriate credit for photographic material. The publisher deeply regrets any omission and pledges to correct errors called to its attention in subsequent editions.

Unless otherwise acknowledged, all photographs are the property of Scott Foresman, a division of Pearson Education.

Photo locators denoted as follows: Top (T), Center (C), Bottom (B), Left (L), Right (R), Background (Bkgd)

Illustrations by Jerry Tiritilli

ISBN 13: 978-0-328-51340-6
ISBN 10:   0-328-51340-7

19 16

My name is Jeannie Grigsby. I want to tell you about my great-great-great-great-uncle, Carl Grigsby. He was born more than 150 years ago, and he was a cowboy.

I've been hearing family stories about Uncle Carl since I was born.

When Carl Grigsby was just sixteen, he went to work for the Lazy L Ranch in Texas. Mr. Tom Lambert, the ranch owner, raised a type of cattle called Texas longhorns.

Carl liked the longhorns. He said they were the best cattle around. They'd eat almost anything that grew.

The flat land all around the ranches was called the range. The range was wide open land. All the ranchers grazed their cattle on the range.

Each rancher put his cowboys in charge of his cattle. The cowboys had to keep their herd together on the range.

Carl and the other cowboys from the Lazy L rode out each morning. They'd watch over the longhorns all day and keep them from mixing with other cattle from a different ranch.

The most important job for cowboys was the trail drive. The trail drive was when a herd of cattle was taken to the closest railroad station. From there, the cattle went east to the market. It sounds like easy work, doesn't it? But it wasn't!

There could be as many as three thousand longhorns on the drive. That's a lot of cattle to watch over! A trail drive was not just a short little trip. At that time the nearest railroad to the Lazy L was in Dodge City, Kansas.

It could take three months to drive the cattle up the trail to Dodge City.

Carl and the rest of the cowboys had to keep the cattle together, headed in the right direction. Some cowboys would lead the way. Others would ride beside and behind the herd.

The cattle raised a lot of dust as they moved along. Carl wore a bandanna to try to keep some of the dust away from his face. But dust was always getting into his eyes.

If you asked Carl, "What's the worst thing that can happen on a cattle drive?" he would probably say, "STAMPEDE!"

A loud sound could sometimes scare the cattle. A clap of thunder would startle them. All of a sudden, they would gallop off in the wrong direction.

The cowboys would have to gallop out and get ahead of the stampede. They could sometimes see the cattle charging right at them!

The cowboys would rise up in their saddles, wave their hats, and shout. This would stop the cattle and make them turn back.

What do you think was the best thing about a trail drive? For Carl it was sitting around the campfire at sunset when the cattle were resting.

The cowboys would cook, eat, talk, and watch the sun go down. Sometimes they would sing songs until midnight.

When Carl had been working for the Lazy L for about ten years, something big happened. Barbed wire was invented.

People could unwind this wire and attach it to fence posts. This made it easy to put up long fences. Soon, ranchers were fencing in their land. The fences kept the cattle together. The ranchers didn't need cowboys to do that job anymore.

The next thing Carl knew, he was out in the hot midday sun pounding fence posts into the ground and stringing barbed wire. He thought fences were a big mistake.

"The range is for everybody," he'd say. "We should keep it open so we can all share it, not fence it in!"

Carl missed the open range, but he still rode on trail drives—until the railroad came to Texas a few years later. There was no need for cattle drives after that. The trains took the cattle to Dodge City without help from the cowboys. The days of the big trail drives were over.

Carl worked around the ranch, taking care of the cattle and fixing the fences that he hated. He didn't feel like a cowboy anymore. He felt useless.

One day, a ranch hand told him about something called a rodeo. It was a kind of show where cowboys showed their skills riding and racing horses, and roping and handling cows and calves.

That sounded like much more fun than fixing fences. Everyone had always told Carl how good he was on a horse. He'd often beaten the other cowboys in races.

Carl Grigsby spent the rest of his life performing in rodeos. When he got too old to perform, he'd come and watch the big rodeos. He'd remember the old days, when he was a real cowboy.

There are still some cattle ranches around today. The people working on ranches rope cattle, fix fences, and take cattle to market. Things are different now than they were in Carl's day.

People use machines to fix the fences. They use trucks to move the cattle. People working on ranches now are called cowhands, not cowboys. A lot more cowhands are women these days.

As for me, I don't know if I'll work on the ranch, but I'll never forget about Carl Grigsby and the rest of the cowboys. Sometimes, I sing a song Carl used to sing, way back when he was still a cowboy. It's about the end of the open range, when the terrible fences came to Texas. It goes like this:

*I'm going to leave
    the old ranch now.
I've got no place
    to roam.
They've roped and fenced
    my cattle range.
And the place don't
    feel like home.*

Rodeos for Kids

Back in the old days, cowboys used to get together and have contests. It was something to do for fun after they got back from a trail drive or after a roundup. Rodeos grew out of these contests. They started in the late 1880s as a place where cowboys could show off their skills to others.

These days, there are cowgirls in rodeos too. There are even some rodeos just for kids! The oldest kids' rodeo is run by an organization called Little Britches. It's for kids from five to eighteen years old. Do you think you would like to try being in a rodeo?